Doctor Who

200 Facts on the Characters and Making of the BBC TV Series

By Andy Bell

As a "thank you" for purchasing this book I want to give you a gift. It is 100% absolutely free.

Please go to http://fandomkindlebooks.com/doctor-who-bonus/ to discover more fascinating facts about 'Doctor Who' and that other worldwide smash hit BBC TV series, 'Sherlock'.

Disclaimer

Table of Contents

Introduction

In a world where interests change in a moment, lasting success is hard to come by.

This is one reason why television shows rarely last longer than a few seasons. Times change, fans move on, and old heroes are abandoned for new characters who connect more with the changing times.

However, there is one series that seems to defy this expectation. Decade after decade, 'Doctor Who' keeps its audience of young and old alike, captivated with its story lines. This series is as much loved now as it was when it first appeared on our screens back in the early 1960s.

A Time Lord travelling throughout space, in his trusted time machine The TARDIS, lends itself to re-invention. Perhaps this is where the staying power of the series lies. Being able to change as times move on and decades pass, means that the Doctor stays fresh in the eyes of his fans.

His adventures stay current, his companions keep him 'on trend,' and each year more and more fans join his ever-growing band of followers.

Forty-two years after the show first appeared, and some 16 years after the previous Doctor had been seen on our TV screens, 'Doctor Who' came back to life in 2005, its instant success confirming that he had been missed. His fans had been loyal and were more than ready to resume his adventures.

Since then, the Doctor has enjoyed a huge resurgence in popularity. Always much loved in the UK, he now enjoys a large fan base worldwide, and especially across the pond in the States.

Come with us as we take a look at the world of the Doctor: who is he, what is he here for, and his most recent incarnations.

If you love the Doctor, then you will love delving into his background to fill in the gaps and find out bits of information that perhaps you didn't know. Maybe you already did. Test how much of a fan you really are by seeing how many of these facts you know.

Whatever your reason for being here, buckle up and enjoy the ride, as we take you on a journey through time and space, into the world of the most recent Doctors, from 2005 to the present day.

In the words of David Tennant, the tenth Doctor, "Allons-y!"

The Recent History of 'Doctor Who'

'Doctor Who' first aired on British TV, on Saturday, 23rd November 1963.

The initial response was poor due to the assassination of President John F Kennedy the day before. However, the episode was repeated the following week before the showing of Episode Two, and with better ratings, the series ran.

It first aired in Northern America, courtesy of the Canadian Network (CBC), on Saturday, 23rd January 1965.

The first Doctor was played by William Hartnell. He portrayed a rather grumpy, elderly Doctor, but despite this, he was popular, and played the role until October 1966.

There have been 12 Doctors in total.

The Doctor is an alien Time Lord, from the planet Gallifrey.

Whilst others of his kind are happy to oversee time and space, the Doctor steals an obsolete time machine and leaves his planet to explore the Universe.

The TARDIS is the Doctor's iconic time machine. One of its best known characteristics is that it is bigger on the inside than the outside.

The TARDIS was modelled on a 1963 British police call box, and has stayed that way ever since.

'Doctor Who' had been intended as an 'educational' program. It was aired at a time when it was thought mainly children would be watching.

Episodes alternated between an episode going back in time (to teach children about history), and an episode going forward in time (to teach children about science).

The popularity of the historic episodes was never as good, and so the decision was made to drop these.

The series was taken off the air in 1989. A TV film was made in 1996, with Paul McGann as the eighth Doctor. It was intended as a backdoor pilot to commission a new series in the States. However, although it did well in the UK, it failed to receive the reviews it needed, and the idea was shelved.

The chief visionary and driving force behind the new series was Russell T Davies. In addition to writing many of the scripts, he was also the executive producer.

Over 90 writers have received on screen credit for writing 'Doctor Who' episodes.

In 2005, for the first time in the program's history, a Christmas Special of 'Doctor Who' was commissioned.

It was decided at the end of the fourth season of the new 'Doctor Who,' to take a hiatus for a year. Instead, several 'specials' were commissioned for that year, at the end of which the tenth Doctor, David Tennant, bowed out.

With several of the production team also moving on to new pastures, it became clear that the fifth season, in 2010, would prove to be a benchmark for the new 'Doctor Who.' A new Doctor and new production team would lead the way into a new decade of adventures for the Doctor.

With the departure of Russell T Davies as Executive Producer, Steven Moffatt stepped in to fill his shoes. Steven Moffatt was later involved with the new series of Sherlock.

Much changed with the start of Season Five. The console room of the TARDIS, and the shell itself were revamped, as the program pushed ahead in new directions.

A special 3D episode, shown in cinemas, was commissioned to celebrate the 50th anniversary of 'Doctor Who' on the 23rd November, 2013.

Matt Smith, the eleventh Doctor, announced he would leave after the Christmas special in 2013.

The role of the twelfth Doctor would now be carried forward by Peter Capaldi.

'Doctor Who' program statistics:

The Ninth Doctor (Christopher Eccleston) 2005: one season, 13 episodes

The Tenth Doctor (David Tennant) 2005 - 2009: three seasons, 42 episodes; 5 specials

The Eleventh Doctor (Matt Smith) 2010 - 2013: three seasons, 42 episodes, 2 specials

'Doctor Who'-Related Trivia

The Daleks first appeared in December 1963, and appeared in 99 episodes in total, up to and including January 2014.

Their catchphrase is 'exterminate'.

A British survey held in 2008, showed that 9 out of 10 UK children could correctly identify a Dalek.

Hiding behind the sofa whenever a Dalek was on TV has become a renowned part of British cultural identity.

K-9 is the robotic dog belonging to the Doctor. If he gets left behind or destroyed, the Doctor simply makes another one. There have been four versions of it so far.

TARDIS stands for 'Time And Relative Dimension In Space'.

The TARDIS was originally designed to take almost any form it wanted. However, due to a faulty chameleon circuit, it got stuck as the 1960s police call box it is now famous for.

The BBC own the patent for the TARDIS, despite the Metropolitan Police filing an objection to the Patent Office. The Patent Office couldn't find any evidence the Metropolitan Police had ever filed to trademark the design, and so ruled in favor of the BBC.

The TARDIS emits a 'wheezing' sound that was originally created by Brian Hodgson, working at the BBC Radiophonic Workshop. He created it by recording a set of house keys being dragged along the strings of an old piano. To this he added echo and reverb effects.

The word TARDIS appears as a word in the Oxford English Dictionary.

The Doctor's ability to regenerate was decided on as a way to overcome the ill-health of the actor William Hartnell. By enabling the Doctor to return as a different actor, it saved the show from being discontinued.

Angry at being blamed for the show's poor ratings, Colin Baker (the sixth Doctor), refused to return and shoot the regeneration scene for the seventh Doctor. As a result, Sylvestor McCoy had to play both Doctors in his opening scene.

Fans lambasted the idea, and it is named as one of the 12 worst deaths in science fiction history.

The famous movie director Ridley Scott was working as a designer at the BBC when the Daleks were due to be designed. He was originally slated for the job, but due to scheduling conflicts, the job went to a colleague instead.

'Doctor Who' outsold US TV's 'Modern Family' and 'Glee' on iTunes in 2011.

The theme tune was the first worldwide to be made up entirely of electronic sounds.

The show is listed in the Guinness Book of World Records as the 'longest running science-fiction TV series'.

The BBC carried out some research in 1972, and found that at that time, 'Doctor Who' was considered to be one of the most violent shows on TV.

Tom Baker was the longest serving Doctor, playing the role from 1974 until 1981.

William Hartnell, the first actor to play the 'Doctor,' was paid 250 guineas (about £260 or $430) for the very first episode in 1963.

A small asteroid belt, asteroid 3325, was discovered in 1984. It was named TARDIS after the Doctor's time/space machine.

The part of River Song, the Doctor's companion in his eleventh incarnation, was originally offered to Kate Winslet. She turned it down and the part went to Alex Kingston.

Many episodes in the 1960s and 1970s were destroyed or wiped by the BBC. This has left a huge gap in the archives of the series, mainly of episodes featuring the first two Doctors.

Actors Bill Nighy and Benedict Cumberbatch both turned down the opportunity to play the Doctor.

Each episode is 45 minutes in length and takes approximately 3 weeks to shoot. The hour-long specials can take up to a month to shoot.

The Ninth Doctor – Christopher Eccleston

Christopher Eccleston made his debut as the ninth Doctor on 26th March 2005.

He is widely credited with helping to re-establish 'Doctor Who,' following its long hiatus.

He says his earliest memory of watching 'Doctor Who' was of Patrick Troughton (the second Doctor) in the late 1960s.

The TARDIS, used by Christopher Eccleston in the first series, sold at auction in 2010 for £10,800 ($18,000).

Eccleston played the Doctor for one series only, a total of 13 episodes.

The ninth Doctor's catchphrase was 'fantastic,' with extra emphasis on the second syllable. It is often said with a trace of irony.

Eccleston's portrayal of the Doctor was moodier, rugged and more streetwise than his predecessors. This helped the character appeal to a new audience who had not seen 'Doctor Who' before.

Eccleston was always writer and producer Russell T Davies' first choice to play the part of the Doctor.

The ninth Doctor is deeply affected by his actions in 'The Last Great Time War'. The weight of destroying both the Time Lords and his own planet weighs heavily on him, leaving him emotionally exhausted.

The ninth incarnation of the Doctor was particularly good at video games.

Unlike his predecessors, the ninth Doctor wears a wrist watch, and often refers to it for the date and year.

Trivia about Christopher Eccleston

Eccleston trained at the Central School of Speech and Drama in London, UK.

He is a committed vegetarian and a very keen runner.

He turned down a role in Stephen Spielberg's 'Saving Private Ryan'.

Unemployed for the first few years after he graduated, Eccleston found himself taking jobs in supermarkets, on building sites, and as an artist's model.

His favorite album is 'What's Going On' by Marvin Gaye.

He starred in the 2001 film 'The Others' alongside Nicole Kidman.

The Ninth Doctor's Companions

Rose Tyler – played by Billie Piper

Rose is an emotional nineteen-year-old, living on a London council estate when the Doctor meets her.

She works in a department store, which has been taken over by an Auton invasion. The Doctor blows the store up, and Rose starts to travel with the Doctor.

Rose was more independent and courageous than the Doctor's previous companions. Eccleston says of her: 'Rose is a heroine, who teaches the Doctor huge emotional lessons'.

Rose is one of the most popular companions.

Eccleston remarked that the relationship between the Doctor and Rose was 'love at first sight'.

However, it was more mysterious than a conventional love affair.

Viewers of the series often remark on the romantic tension between Rose and the Doctor.

Prior to this series of 'Doctor Who,' companions never got romantically involved with the Doctor, so this was a significant departure from the established norm.

Adam Mitchell – played by Bruno Langley

Adam joins the Doctor and Rose in the episode 'Dalek' and stays for just a single episode.

Russell T Davies wrote the part of Adam to show that not all companions were good ones. He is dubbed 'the companion who couldn't'.

Upon returning Adam to his home, the Doctor tells him 'I only take the best. I've got Rose'.

Jack Harkness – played by John Barrowman

Jack joins the Doctor and Rose in the episode 'The Empty Child' in May 2005.

He appears in 11 episodes in total and appears in the spin-off series 'Torchwood'.

An ex-con artist and time agent, he becomes immortal after Rose brings him back to life using the Time Vortex.

Although Jack is friendly and very flirtatious, he is also ruthless, and will not hesitate to kill anyone who stands in his way or who he feels is a threat.

The Tenth Doctor – David Tennant

David Tennant took over the role of the Doctor in the 'Parting of The Ways' in June 2005.

He played the role for 5 years, until the episode 'The End of Time,' in January 2010.

Widely considered to be one of the best Doctors, Tennant's incarnation of Doctor Who further cemented the popularity of the 'new' 'Doctor Who'.

The tenth Doctor comes across as easy-going, chatty and cheeky in nature. However, as with all his previous incarnations, he hides profound anger and regret, which bubble up from time to time.

Tennant's Doctor battles against loneliness. His companions are short-lived, and often meet with tragedy.

Unlike previous incarnations, the tenth Doctor is something of a romantic and a ladies' man.

The obvious mutual affection between Rose and the Doctor continues with the tenth incarnation. However, it remains unspoken between them.

In the episode 'The Time Crash,' Tennant's Doctor comes into confrontation with his fifth incarnation, played by Peter Davison. This marks the first time in the new series that two incarnations of the Doctor appear face-to-face.

During an interview with chat show host Parkinson, Russell T. Davies and Tennant admitted that the style of the tenth Doctor was taken from an outfit worn by the chef Jamie Oliver, when he had previously appeared on Parkinson.

Tennant won a National Television award in 2007 for his role as the Doctor.

In a real-life twist of fate, in 2011 Tennant married Georgia Moffett. Georgia not only plays the daughter of the tenth Doctor in the episode 'The Doctor's Daughter,' but she is also the real-life daughter of Peter Davison, who played the fifth Doctor.

Playing the Doctor was the fulfillment of a childhood dream for Tennant. In a radio interview on the subject, he remarked 'Who wouldn't want to be the Doctor?'

Tennant's Doctor favors certain phrases, such as 'Brilliant,' 'Oh yes' and 'I'm sorry, I'm so sorry'.

The tenth Doctor has a love for human popular culture such as Harry Potter and The Lion King.

Trivia about David Tennant

Tennant graduated from the Royal Scottish Academy of Music and Drama.

He decided to become an actor at the age of 3.

His real name is David McDonald. However, when he came he to enroll in the actors' union, Equity, he learned there was already a David McDonald registered. He decided to change his name to Tennant after reading an interview with Neil Tennant, lead singer with the British pop group 'The Pet Shop Boys'.

He is a big fan of the film director Alfred Hitchcock.

He says that his favorite Doctor was that of Tom Baker, the fourth Doctor.

He claims he started acting with the hope that one day he would get to play the Doctor.

The Tenth Doctor's Companions

Rose Tyler – played by Billie Piper

Although initially unsure of the Doctor's regeneration, Rose grows even fonder of the tenth Doctor. The chemistry is stronger than it was with his ninth incarnation, and he appears happier.

At the end of the episode, 'Army of Ghosts/Doomsday,' Rose is forced to escape to a parallel universe with her mother. A rich, entrepreneur version of her father lives on in this universe. Here, Rose starts work for the Torchwood Institute.

Rose later returns in the episode, 'The Stolen Earth/Journey's End,' to help save the Earth from the Daleks. During the battle, a half-Time Lord, half-human version of the Doctor is created. After winning the battle, Rose and the half-human Doctor return to the parallel universe together.

Rose's boyfriend, Mickey Smith, appears in several episodes and joins a group of time travelers from a parallel universe.

Donna Noble – played by Catherine Tate

Although Donna appears in the closing scene of the episode, 'Doomsday,' it is not until the episode, 'Runaway Bride,' that we get to meet her properly.

Appearing suddenly in her wedding dress in the TARDIS, it becomes apparent that her fiancé is working for the Racnoss Empress in a bid to defeat the Earth. Donna helps the Doctor defeat the Empress, but declines his invitation to travel with him.

Donna later has a change of heart, returns to the Doctor, and travels with him through the entirety of series eight.

In her final scenes of 'Journey's End,' Donna touches the Doctor's energized and severed hand, and her mind becomes filled with the totality of his knowledge. Proving too much for her mind to cope with, the Doctor is forced to wipe her memory in order to save her.

From that moment on, Donna has no memory of her time with the Doctor, the adventures they shared, nor the lives they saved.

The Doctor says this of Donna, 'But for one moment, one shining moment, she was the most important woman in the whole wide Universe'.

Martha Jones – played by Freema Agyeman

Martha and the Doctor meet in the episode 'Smith and Jones,' when the Doctor saves the hospital that Martha is working in.

The Doctor invites Martha to travel with him, making sure to tell her that she will not be a replacement for Rose. Martha agrees when she learns that she can return to her life without losing any time.

Together they share many adventures (spread over 19 episodes on 'Doctor Who' and 3 on 'Torchwood'), before she realizes that her love for him will always remain unrequited. Unable to continue traveling, and not wanting to go back to her former life, the Doctor recommends for her to work at UNIT. This is a military organisation, set up to investigate and eliminate both paranormal and extra-terrestrial threats.

The Eleventh Doctor – Matt Smith

Matt Smith takes on the role of the eleventh Doctor from 'The End of Time,' in January 2010, until the Christmas special 'The Time of the Doctor,' in December 2013.

The eleventh incarnation of the Doctor is lively, energetic and eccentric. Resourceful and quick thinking, he is able to spin most situations around to his point of view. Much like his previous incarnation, the tenth Doctor, he is able to find the positives in most negative situations.

This incarnation of the Doctor hates distractions when he is trying to work out a problem. Instead, he likes to have those around him focus on survival.

He declares, 'Patience is for wimps'. He finds that he has to try harder than his previous incarnations to stay busy, as boredom makes him lose his mind.

Like his second incarnation, this Doctor also has a childlike recklessness about him. However, he always has a grand plan behind his actions.

He has a habit of referring to his companions by their surname. The first incarnation of the Doctor did this as well. However, in the case of the eleventh Doctor, it is more a sign of affection than a way to annoy.

Writer Steven Moffat describes Matt Smith's Doctor as 'An old man in a young man's body'.

Smith himself, says of the Doctor, 'He is someone with a lot of blood on his hands. This is one of the reasons that he travels constantly and loves the thrill of adventure'.

Matt owns the tweed jacket that his eleventh Doctor wears.

He was the first lead actor in 'Doctor Who' to be nominated for a BAFTA Best Actor TV Award.

The classic series of 'Doctor Who' ended without Matt watching it. Therefore, unlike his predecessor, David Tennant, he was not a fan of the show when he took on the role.

During his final episode 'The Time of The Doctor,' it is revealed that the Doctor has used all his regenerations, and that he is, in fact, in his thirteenth and final body. This explains his aged appearance throughout this episode.

At the end of this episode the Time Lords grant the Doctor a new regeneration cycle.

Writer Steven Moffat hailed Matt's final performance of the Doctor as 'Heartbreakingly good'.

Trivia about Matt Smith

He was a talented soccer player as a teenager and had dreams of turning professional. However, a back injury led him to give it up, and he turned to acting instead.

He can play the guitar.

Smith studied drama and creative writing at the University of East Anglia in Norwich, UK.

He is well known among his co-stars and the crew for being incredibly clumsy. Producers often take bets on how long it will take him to break a prop.

He insisted his Doctor wear the bow tie that became the trademark of the eleventh Doctor.

His nickname is 'Smithers'.

The Companions of the Eleventh Doctor

Amelia 'Amy' Pond – played by Karen Gillian

Amy and the Doctor first meet in the episode 'The Eleventh Hour'. Amy is disturbed by a crack in her bedroom wall. This turns out to be one of several cracks in the Universe.

The Doctor leaves to save the Earth, but promises to return to Amy within 5 minutes and take her travelling with him. However, due to a fault with the TARDIS, he actually returns twelve years later.

After travelling with the Doctor for some time, Amy reveals that she left the Earth on the eve of her wedding to Rory Williams. She then attempts to seduce the Doctor. His response is to find Rory and reunite the two. After a while, Amy realizes that it is really Rory that she loves.

Rory Williams – played by Arthur Darvill

Rory chooses to join Amy and the Doctor as a travel companion and he and Amy eventually marry.

They later discover their fellow travel companion, River Song, is actually their daughter who had been kidnapped as a baby.

Amy and Rory have many adventures with the Doctor, and star in many of the episodes from 2010 through to 2012.

River Song – played by Alex Kingston

River Song is the daughter of Amy Pond and Rory Williams. She was conceived aboard the TARDIS, which has given her genetic traits and abilities similar to the Time Lords.

Kidnapped as a baby, she is trained by 'The Silence,' a race of hypnotic aliens, to assassinate the Doctor.

Because she is also a time traveller, her meetings with the Doctor appear out of synch, but her story is eventually pieced together.

Having fallen in love with the Doctor, River Song doesn't want to kill him. She has no choice though and after marrying him, has to kill him. It is later revealed that the Doctor she married and killed was simply a double, and the real Doctor had already got away.

The tenth Doctor only meets her in the two-part story, 'Silence in the Library'/'Forest of the Dead,' in which she dies.

Because her timeline does not occur chronologically, when she meets the Doctor for the first time, the Doctor meets her for the last time; when she meets

the Doctor for the last time, he meets her for the first
time.

Clara Oswald – played by Jenna Coleman

Clara is introduced to viewers twice before her
official debut as the latest Doctor Who companion.
Originally we meet her as Oswin Oswald, the only
survivor of the *Starship Alaska*. She dies in the
process of helping the Doctor (Matt Smith) and his
companions (Amy and Rory) escape.

Later we are introduced to her as Clara, a barmaid
and governess in Victorian England, who is set to
become the new companion, but who dies before she
does so.

Finally, her character is established in modern
day, and she joins him as a plucky, go-getting
woman who, in Matt Smith's final episode,

persuades the Time Lords to save him. They allow him another regeneration, and Peter Capaldi arrives.

Jenna Coleman auditioned for the role of Clara in secret. She auditioned for "Men On Waves" which is an anagram for "Woman Seven".

The Twelfth Doctor – Peter Capaldi

Capaldi had already played three roles within the 'Doctor Who' franchise, before he was given the role of the Doctor. He played a brief cameo role in the 50th Anniversary episode 'The Day of The Doctor.' He appeared in the role of the twelfth Doctor officially on the 25th December 2013, when Matt Smith's Doctor regenerated. He also appeared as the character Carciluis in the 2008 episode 'The Fires of Pompeii.'

When he was cast at 55 years of age, Capaldi was the same age as the first Doctor, William Hartnell.

When Jon Pertwee was playing the third Doctor, the then-teenage Capaldi wrote and sent scripts to the production offices of 'Doctor Who'. Barry Letts began to write to Capaldi, which resulted in an invitation to come and visit Pertwee and the studios. Capaldi later claimed that this incident

was instrumental in his decision to become an
actor.

Trivia about Peter Capaldi

Capaldi was the lead singer of a punk rock group called 'Dreamboys.' Its line-up included the comedian Craig Ferguson, who went on to host a talk show in America.

Prior to being cast as the twelfth Doctor, Capaldi had a part in the Brad Pitt blockbuster 'World War Z.' His character was called the W.H.O. Doctor.

He has a role in the upcoming Angelina Jolie film 'Maleficent'.

Like David Tennant, Capaldi claims he is a lifelong 'Doctor Who' fan.

He won an Oscar in 1995 for Best Director for a 'Live Action Short Film' for "Franz Kafka's It's a Wonderful Life".

He has said of 'Doctor Who', 'Being asked to play the Doctor was a huge privilege. I find myself in a state of utter terror and delight. I can't wait to get started'.

Arch-Enemies of Doctor Who

The Daleks

The main arch-enemies of Doctor Who have to be the Daleks. An extraterrestrial race of cyborgs, they were created by the scientist Davros during the final years of the thousand year war with the Thals.

Davros integrated his own genetically modified race with a tank-like robot to create the Dalek.

As an added modification, he removed the ability to feel compassion, pity and remorse.

The Daleks quickly came to see themselves as the supreme race of the Universe.

Their intense hatred leaves them with a singular desire to purge the Universe of all non-Dalek life forms.

During a battle with the Time Lords, they were almost wiped out. This happens between the 1996 TV film and the start of the new series in 2005. However, the event is referenced in the 50th Anniversary episode 'The Day of the Doctor'.

The Master

The Master is a renegade Time Lord and archenemy of the Doctor.

Like the Doctor, The Master has the ability to regenerate. Hence, he has been played by many different actors over the years.

The team behind 'Doctor Who' created The Master as a recurring villain, much like Moriarty is to Sherlock Holmes.

The Doctor and The Master are of similar intelligence, and were classmates on Gallifrey.

The Master's sole desire is to conquer and control the Universe. Second to this is his wish to destroy or hurt The Doctor.

The Doctor assumes The Master is dead, as after the 'Last Great Time War,' it is stated that the Doctor is the sole surviving Time Lord. However, it is later revealed that The Master is still alive. The Doctor receives a message in the episode 'Gridlock' that simply states, 'You are not alone'.

The Cybermen

This race of cyborgs are among the most persistent of the Doctors enemies.

They were originally an organic species of humanoid. However, in an attempt at self-preservation, they added more and more artificial parts to themselves. This leaves them cold, calculating, logical, and devoid of any emotion.

They have been featured many times in the classic series. Since the show's revival, the Cybermen have returned in a parallel universe.

A further redesign in 2013 sees them as technologically advanced enough to instantly upgrade themselves, fixing flaws and defects.

While the Daleks remain virtually unchanged, the Cybermen seem to change at every encounter, making them increasingly difficult to defeat.

Their main weakness is gold. While their armor can withstand bullets, it can be penetrated by gold arrows or other gold projectiles.

While the Daleks, The Master and Cybermen are three of the more well-known of the Doctor's enemies, there have been many, many others over the years. Listed below are just some that you may have come across:

The Silence

The Silence is a religious order with the sole intention of killing the Doctor. They seek to prevent anyone asking the question 'Doctor Who?'

The Sontarans

The Doctor has encountered the Sonatarans many times over his travels. Their lives are dedicated to battle and war against the Rutans.

The Rutans

Rutans resemble giant green jelly fish who can speak. They have advanced shape-shifting abilities and are ingenious spies.

The Zygons

The Zygons only appeared in one 1975 episode, although they did appear in the 50th Anniversary Special. They are an alien, shape-shifting race that can take the form of other beings.

The Ice Warriors

The Ice Warriors are reptilian humanoids that come from the planet Mars. They are tall, with scaly skin, and speak with a long, drawn-out hiss.

The Autons

The Nesteric Consciousness have the ability to control plastic, and have been colonizing planets for millions of years. They create living plastic dummies, known as Autons, for this purpose.

Sulurians and Sea Devils

The Sulurians are a race of technologically-advanced humanoid reptiles. They once ruled during prehistoric times.

Sea Devils are cousins of the Sulurians, and are amphibious in nature.

The Weeping Angels

First appearing in 2007, The Weeping Angels are one of the Doctor's most feared enemies. An ancient race dating back to the start of the

Universe, they move quickly and silently when not seen. When seen, they turn to stone statues until the person looks away, and they can move again.

The 'Doctor Who' Spin-off Series, 'Torchwood'

Created by Russell T Davies, 'Torchwood' follows the exploits of a Cardiff-based institute and its small team of alien hunters.

The Torchwood Institute was created by Queen Victoria in 1879.

Its mission was to safeguard the British Isles from extraterrestrial activity and to capture alien technology for the good of the empire.

The lead character is Captain Jack Harkness, who originally appeared in the 2005 series of 'Doctor Who.'

In series one and two, the show uses a 'time rift' in Cardiff. This helps account for the unusually high number of aliens in Cardiff.

In the third and fourth series, the members of Torchwood operate as fugitives. In the third series, they run out of London, and in the fourth, they end up operating out of the United States.

There is an unofficial slogan within Torchwood that says, 'If it's alien, it's ours'.

The name 'Torchwood' is an anagram of 'Doctor Who'.

'Torchwood' is considered the 'adult' version of 'Doctor Who'.

All four series of 'Torchwoood' have aired overseas in Asia, Australia, New Zealand, Europe and North America. However, in October 2012, Davies announced that for personal reasons, the show would take an indefinite hiatus.

The 50th Anniversary Special – 'The Day of The Doctor'

On the 23rd November 2013, a special 50th anniversary episode of 'Doctor Who' aired. It was entitled 'The Day of The Doctor'.

Written by Steven Moffat, it was shown in both 2D and 3D.

The episode achieved a Guinness World Record for the largest-ever simulcast of a TV drama show.

The episode follows the events of the last day of the 'Last Great Time War'. It had previously been thought that the Doctor destroyed his home planet of Gallifrey.

Over the course of the episode, it becomes apparent that the Doctors, following a companion's plea, change their minds. Instead of destroying the planet, they place it in a frozen moment of time.

In order not to disturb the flow of time, all of the Doctors but the eleventh, upon returning to their timelines, forget the alternate ending to the Time War.

The episode starred the eleventh Doctor, Matt Smith, and his companion, Clara Oswald, played by Jenna Coleman.

Two other Doctors show up for the episode. The tenth Doctor, played by David Tennant, and The War Doctor, played by John Hurt.

Also making a re-appearance in the episode was Billie Piper, who instead of reprising her role of Rose, plays a sentient doomsday weapon called The Moment. She is invisible and inaudible to everyone but the War Doctor.

The Moment doomsday weapon, due to being left unattended for such a long time, has developed its own conscience. In this special, it takes the form of Rose.

Tom Baker, the actor who played the fourth Doctor, makes an uncredited appearance as the curator. His likeness to the fourth Doctor is alluded to but not explained.

David Tennant and Matt Smith had so much fun working together on the special episode that they came up with plans to do it again. Sadly, the producers were not so keen on further episodes, but admitted that they were 'absolutely adorable and hilarious together'.

Conclusion

'Doctor Who' has become a household name over the 50 years that it has been running.

It has somehow found a successful niche to sit in, one that appeals to each generation of children as much as the next. These children grow up to be fans as adults too, watching as they introduce their children to the Doctor.

If you were a child of the 60s and 70s, then you will have grown up with the Daleks, and 'hiding behind the sofa' on a Saturday night was almost a rite of passage. Children today will grow up with different memories of the Doctor, memories that will be no less strong.

Peter Capaldi, the twelfth Doctor, summed it up when he said this:

"The big reason that 'Doctor Who' is still with us is that every single viewer who ever turned on to watch this show, at any age, at any time in its history, took it into their heart -- because 'Doctor Who' belongs to all of us. Everyone made 'Doctor Who'."

Never before has a television program captured the imagination in the way that 'Doctor Who' has.

Its success doesn't lie with the good fortune of the writers in finding a way to bring the story through the decades. Nor does it matter that the special effects and aliens are now more realistic than ever. Even having actors who are current and well-known to the younger viewers isn't the key to its long-lasting appeal.

What matters is The Doctor. We can identify with him. He is no super hero. In fact, he is something of a 'geek,' a 'nerd' with bad dress sense. Despite this, or perhaps because of it, he has become one of us over the decades. He gets angry and frustrated, and often struggles to make sense of his circumstances. However, he is also fiercely loyal to those he loves, and tries to see the positive in everything.

These are attributes that are easy to identify with. He is real, and this is where his strength lies.

However old or young you are, whatever part of his history resonates most with you, Peter Capaldi was right: Doctor Who belongs to all of us.

Don't forget to claim your free gift!

As a 'thank you' for purchasing this book I want to give you a gift. It is 100% absolutely free.

Please go to http://fandomkindlebooks.com/doctor-who-bonus/ to discover more fascinating facts about 'Doctor Who' and that other worldwide smash hit BBC TV series, 'Sherlock'.

Made in the USA
Middletown, DE
14 December 2014